Examination Centre

Other poetry titles by the same author

The Pond
Shadowboxing
On Holy Week

Examination Centre

poems

MERVYN MORRIS

New Beacon Books Ltd
London ● Port of Spain

First published in 1992 by New Beacon Books Ltd,
76 Stroud Green Road, London N4 3EN, England.

© 1992 Mervyn Morris

ISBN 1873201 08 7 (hardback)
      1873201 09 5 (paperback)

All rights reserved. No part of this publication may be reproduced or transmitted in any form or by any means, electronic or mechanical, including photography, recording or any information storage or retrieval system, without prior permission in writing from the publisher.

Printed by Villiers Publications Ltd., 19 Sylvan Avenue, London N3 2LE, England.

for **Helen**

ACKNOWLEDGEMENTS

Some of these poems have appeared in the following journals and newspapers: *Jamaica Journal, Pathways, The Sunday Gleaner, Public Opinion, Bim, Kykoveral, Trinidad and Tobago Review, Race Today, The Times Literary Supplement, Ariel, Cincinnati Poetry Review, Graham House Review, Greenfield Review, International Portland Review.*

CONTENTS

Examination Centre	9
Literary Evening, Jamaica	10
Question Time	11
Web	12
Writing	13
She	14
Living Near the Zoo	15
Going Through the Park	16
Snapshot	17
Acrobat	18
Night Flight	19
Home	20
Presences	21
Games	22
Interlude	23
Love Is	24
Peacetime	25
Version	26
Recreation	27
Guinea-pig	28
Memento	29
Epiphany	30
Sister	31
Seen	32
The Militant	33
Why, This Is Hull	34
Jamaica 1979	35
Scorpions	36
Riding Hood: Version	37
There Was a Young Poet	38
Some Epigrams	39
Fable	40
Fete	41
On Campus, Murder	42
Meeting the Mage	43
Data	44
Teacher	45
My Rodney Poem	46
Omens	47
Historian	48
Departure Lounge	49
Windscreen	50
Legion	51
Walk Good	52

EXAMINATION CENTRE

Dilapidated room,
paint peeling.
Sufferers
on edge.

The chief invigilator
gives the word.
The fingered papers rustle.

Outside the centre –
part of my recall –
trees bend and stretch
and breathe.
Winds, playful, tease.

We're struggling here
with questions
and time
and longing
for a life we glimpse
through dust
clouding the panes.

LITERARY EVENING, JAMAICA

In a dusty old crumbling building just fit for rats
And much too large for precious poetry circles
The culture fans sat scattered in the first ten rows
Listening for English poetry.

Geoff read Larkin beautifully, Enright too,
And Michael Saunders talked between the poems:
"I don't say they are wonderful," he said,
"And would not say that anybody says
They're great. I offer them
As two fair English poets writing nowadays.
They're anti-gesture, anti-flatulence,
They speak their quiet honesties without pretence."

The longer section of the evening's programme
Was poems by the locals, undergraduates,
Some coarse, some wild, and many violent,
All bloody with the strains of rape and childbirth,
Screaming hot curses anti-slavery,
"Down with the limey bastards! Up the blacks!
Chr-rist! Let's tear the painted paper
Off all the blasted cracks!"

The more I heard the more it seemed
A pretty rotten choice to read us Larkin,
Dull-mannered, scared, regressive Phil,
Saying No to everything or Soon, Not Yet.
So many bulging poets must have blushed
And wondered where the hell they'd ever get
With noisy poems, brash, self-conscious, colourful,
And feared that maybe they were born too crude.
Maybe they were: but it was bloody rude
Seeming to ask for things that don't belong out here
Where sun shines hot and love is plentiful.

For to us standing here, a naked nation
Bracing ourselves for blows, what use
Is fearfulness and bland negation?
What now if honesty should choose
To say, in all this world's confusion,
That we are still too young for disillusion?

QUESTION TIME

sometimes a poem
is a mask

to ritualize
connection

& preserve
a little something

shared a little
something treasured

in pretence
that privacy

lives on within
community

WEB

skeins of
perception
catching
light

gossamer
filaments
of radiating
glances

please
do not touch

WRITING
(after Octavio Paz)

When in some solitary hour
pen writes on paper
who makes it move?
Who is he writing to, writing for me
this littoral of lips, of dream,
this shoulder to forget the world forever on?

Someone inside me writes, he moves my hand,
selects a word, then pauses, wavering
between green mountains and blue sea.
Coldly examines what I write,
dashes it in the fire.
But this judge is a victim who,
condemning me, condemns himself.
He writes nobody, calls nobody,
he writes himself, gets lost inside himself,
and finds himself again, once more becoming me.

SHE

tangling
with undergrowth
he hears

her questioning
the twilight
fears

summoning softly
into jungle
into night

LIVING NEAR THE ZOO

resentfully awake
inside our bungalows

we hear
the cinematic roar of lions
in their cages

GOING THROUGH THE PARK

Out of the shadow an awkward figure
loomed, commanding, with a gun.
The finger tightened on the trigger.

The finger tightened on the trigger.
She couldn't fight, she couldn't run;
she learned in that peculiar park
how much she feared the gun.

The finger tightened on the trigger.
Then suddenly along the dark
gun-muzzle whoosh! a full balloon
came rushing, rainbow-bright!

The awkward figure laughed. And soon
that weird encounter faded into night.

ACROBAT

brave woman

   trusting
he has gauged

her arc
exactly

she's letting go
    she's flying

in the dark

SNAPSHOT

i press your eyes
and study the exposure
in my head
i have you
sagging in a rumpled bed
(dont go dont go)

one snapshot
in the miles & miles
of undeveloped
yesterdays

(shutter your gaze)

NIGHT FLIGHT

He's off into the night
alone, the lucky devil –
no one hanging on his tail
to keep him out of trouble.

He flaps his wings
in the uncaged air
and, floating on the night,
is gliding everywhere,

is revelling in flight –
until he feels
the fish-hook in the flesh,
the line tugged tight.

HOME

Father, given a chance to be
away awhile, be free
a month or two,
was quick to grab it!

But freedom's
neither here nor there:
home is the habit
he will always wear.

PRESENCES

You're here.
I conjure you
house-coated, half-asleep
in the armchair by the window.

Awake in bed
I hug you, memory.
They who one another keepe
Alive, ne'r parted bee.

GAMES

Sometimes
when he teetered
on the brink

the woman
saddled with
his mind

would wish him dead
then pray
he'd come again
to safety
and her bed

Time after time
he sidled back
into her care

contending
there was nothing
in the world
to fear

INTERLUDE

Life of the party, he's
a clown on springs

until the keeper
puts him down.

Jack in the box
again, recoiling.

Quick, now!
Click.

LOVE IS

a giving
& a measured taking

amputation
re-creating

everlasting
interface

a prison
& an open space

a teasing glimpse
of holy grail

a generator
that can fail

the naked jugular
the knife

the torsion
balance in my life

PEACETIME

bomb-disposal
combed the area
& declared it clean

but love i cannot
guarantee
safe conduct

through the rubble
of my dreams –

i've read
too many people
blown to bits

by land mines
lying silent
in the dust

long after
all those bells
& all that joy

long after solemn treaties
had been signed & sealed

VERSION

"A marvellous otaheite
dark and sweet,"
the Lord said.
"Eat;
and every time you go to it
the apple will be whole."
Adam loved the apple
heart and soul

until he fancied
on another tree
another apple, dark
(and sweet, presumably).
He checked it.
He enjoyed the change,
the pleasure of the new fruit
succulent and strange.

Eventually remembering
his sweet original,
he turned again and found
a change more radical:
he bit it, and a huge hole gaped:
the thing had lost its power:
his luscious apple now
was withering and sour.

RECREATION

He didn't spend six whole days on the world,
he made it in a single night
when things were not going well and, having hurled
several bad copies into the abyss,
he poured himself some nectar and created this
when he was feeling playful, having got half-tight.

GUINEA-PIG

susceptible
to viruses

that bother
human beings

& therefore
used

as a laboratory
animal

he seldom
bites

he's almost
human:

gentle
stupid

animal
caged

MEMENTO

a wrinkled head
carved sideways
on a hump

a wooden figure
old as sin

it fell from me

& the old man
broke his neck

i left the pieces
   in the garbage
at the railway station

EPIPHANY

your eyes
bright headlights
dip

& we flash by –

SISTER

beneath the undulating
calm
dark currents move

recalling
hurt & rage
& fracture

o my romantic soul
sister longing
for a whole

new world of love
i hear your soft song
breaking on the page

SEEN

beyond the longing
& the lies

half-hidden in
equivocating eyes

(be careful
if you cant be good)

a cringing dread
of being

understood

THE MILITANT

was into painting
butterflies

& now
is into jackboots

stomping painters
painting butterflies

WHY, THIS IS HULL

on a grey day
(spring) when

on my balcony
beyond plate glass

pigeons
flutter & strut

i wing
a little something

to my sun

JAMAICA 1979

a stone's throw
from the revolutionary
slogans on the wall

an old black woman
scavenging
in ruins

Cars idle
at the traffic lights
waiting for green

SCORPIONS

"Sometimes when it was hot as hell
we'd go and capture scorpions for laughs.
Digging a trench around a little circle
where we dumped the heap of them
we'd pour in kerosene and light a fire.
Was fun to watch the devils
eat each other or fry themselves
in trying to escape. Scorpions
are such beasts."

RIDING HOOD: VERSION

he seemed a proper granny
till she grasped the truth –

beneath the pretty bonnet
lay a well-hung youth

working up a story
that he wanted read

with the happy ending
of her maidenhead

THERE WAS A YOUNG POET

There was a young poet
who thrived on his pain
(Hey ho the sun and the rain)
His woman ran off
and he found her again
(Hey ho the sun and the rain)

It pleased him to ask for
a foot in the face
(Hey ho the sun and the rain)
Whenever it hurt enough
words fell in place
(with a Hey ho the sun and the rain)

It happened one summer
nobody knows why
(Hey ho the sun and the rain)
The woman he said he loved
happened to die
(Hey ho the sun and the rain)

He wrote and he wrote
it was his way to grieve
(with a Hey ho the sun and the rain)
The pleasure grief gave him
you wouldn't believe
(Hey ho the sun and the rain)

At length when the sorrow
began to wear thin
(Hey ho the sun and the rain)
He went out and brought
a new torturess in
(Hey ho the sun and the rain)

Turned out she loved him
he found out too late
(Hey ho the sun and the rain)
He's happy as hell
but he cannot create
(Hey ho the sun and the rain)

SOME EPIGRAMS

Beholders

He grew a beard.
They laughed.

And when
he cut it off
they laughed again.

Maverick

They charged him with a lack of guts
and still he wouldn't do as they desired;
to all their quick solutions offering "buts"
instead of the agreement they required.

They dropped him from the inner group –
achieving thus consensus of a fashion.
The relics were a loyal group
who could be certified for passion.

Future Shock

Vociferously critical,
he vanished in the night;
belatedly political,
we know now he was right.

Last Laugh

Dying of a malignant tumor,
he still retained his sense of humour.

FABLE

The grey beast, smiling,
stretched a claw
to draw the artist in;
red with rage
the artist turned and spat.

"I cannot stand
the grey beast
with its coat and tie.
Leave me
to rear my roses
shape opinions
suffer books
paint pictures
love the people
choose true friends."

The grey beast, placid, smiled.

The artist,
red with rage,
fired arrows
at the huge grey gut.

The grey beast, mocking, smiled.

Then one day when the artist dared
to turn and ask for help,
the grey beast muttered sadly,
"You despise me. Help yourself."

FETE

Look that fellow how he staring
at the boys in the band
with a half-empty beer-bottle
dangling from he hand.

Hooked, man, gasping for air
and posing casual, he frown
then suck the beer
and rest the bottle down.

Room full of empties.

ON CAMPUS, MURDER

The gentlemen were rough
trade, and the world closed in
on you, grabbing, jabbing
in the eye, the belly of
your need. Kindness
was never enough.

Koo deh. Him dead fi true.
Sunhot and the glare
of strangers
drilling through
pretences,
a swarm of judges
rubbishing
your delicate defences.

MEETING THE MAGE

Charming, malicious, brilliant,
you posed your aching heart upon your sleeve
(yet so discreetly), breathing warm
to those who loved your sunshine humour,
passionate contempt, your well-turned
praises, witty mimicry –
oh, you were quite a boy, without conceit.

Yet, though so often self-deflating,
you held court all day long. I loved it.
While I was there I loved it; but,
free from that bright ambience,
irony, my cancer, spread.

DATA

facts lie
behind the poems
which are true
fictions

TEACHER
(for Bill Carr, 1931-1992)

Your foreign intervention helped
identify our region. We
give thanks (now you have left us)
finally.

Remembering you, I celebrate
imprudent anger. I commemorate
your obstinate anxiety to share.
True men, you tried to teach us, show they care.

MY RODNEY POEM
*(for Eddie Baugh;
& in memory of Walter, 1942–1980)*

I
He lived
a simple life

He was a man
who cared
when anybody hurt
not just the wretched
of the earth

He dared
to be involved
in nurturing
upheavals

II
Frustrated by
the host of evils
he seemed to me a good
man reaching for the moon

He died
too soon

OMENS

last night
a dream of feasting

today at noon
a green limb broken
in the wind

HISTORIAN
*(for Elsa Goveia,
1925-1980)*

& here we are
remembering
the dark

woman who
searched out meaning
in the dust

& left us
the enigma of her
going

DEPARTURE LOUNGE

The young man,
when the flight is called,
is blowing his nose to clear
the sadness of departure.
The girl who's leaving looks
composed. They're travelling
on different planes
to different destinations.

Each time
we die a little.
When we are young
these moments
devastate.

But partings down the years
have helped to make me
ready to say goodbye.

WINDSCREEN

De garage people
seh de neat
crack in mi windscreen
bound to grow

an though it hardly showin
now, between vibration an de heat
it noh mus grow?

I climb inside
an measure. So I know:
de crack is growin.